Religions of the World for Kids

By

Shalu Sharma

ISBN-13: 978-1500751067

ISBN-10: 1500751065

Publisher: CreateSpace Independent Publishing Platform, North Charleston, SC

Table of contents

What is religion?

Religion is nothing more than a series of beliefs that explain the nature of the world and the purpose of living. Some people think that the point of any religion is simply to govern people and the way they live their lives. But religion helps us to understand the world around us, the purpose of life, things we don't understand, gives us values, explains sufferings and help us to create a better society.

Civil rights activist and a Baptist minister Martin Luther King Jr, said these worlds on the role of religion in society:

"A religion true to its natures must also be concerned about man's social conditions. Religion deals with both earth and heaven, both time and eternity. Religion operates not only on the vertical plane but also on the horizontal. It seeks not only to integrate men with God but to integrate men with men and each man with himself."

The author of this book visiting a church

All the religions of the world were created by man. The men who created these religions were usually prophets that claimed to have spoken with God. These prophets claimed God chose them, so that they could spread his message to other people. In the beginning, prophets would just preach the word of God to people. Then they started writing down God's words into something that is called a "Holy Book." This book is meant to serve as God's guide on how to live our lives and treat other people. Most religions have holy books while others have scriptures or other forms of written documentation regarding the ways of that religion. If you look at the Christian religion, they use a "Holy Bible" to read God's words. As for the Islamic religion, they use a book called the "Quran." Religions all have their own versions of a holy book, which preaches different beliefs and teachings about the world.

Religion is still very active in our modern world. When religions were first created they were used to explain scientific questions, like why someone got sick or where does the sun go at night. Now we have modern day science to explain these things, so religion does not play a big part in that anymore. Still, many people choose to believe in religious teachings because they give them hope about their lives and their future. The religion that people choose to believe in typically has to do with the country or culture they were brought up in. If you were born in the United States then you are typically going to be either a Christian or Judaist because the majority of American citizens belong to one of those religious groups. If you were born in India then you will likely be a Hindu or a Buddhist in Tibet.

Hindus worshipping in a temple

Religion is typically brought to our lives when we are just a child, so we don't have a true saying as to what religion we want to believe in at that age. As people become adults though, they tend to change their religious beliefs as they start to mix with other cultures and learn about other teachings. The true beauty of religion is the freedom to choose your own religion when you are able to.

Types of religion

There are typically two different categories that a religion can fall into, which are monotheistic and polytheistic. A monotheistic religion is any religion that believes or worships only one type of God. There are many popular religions that fit into this category, such as Christianity, Islam and Judaism.

Sign asking worshippers not to talk or sleep in a Buddhist temple

Followers of these religions believe in the words of a single God that got told to a prophet. A polytheistic religion believes and worships more than one god. The three biggest religions that are polytheistic are Hinduism, Buddhism and the Japanese religion known as "Shintoism." Many wars and battles have been fought by various religious groups around the world in the name of religion. They fight because one religious group that has different beliefs than another religious group will feel threatened by them. So, they end up going to war over their own beliefs because they think they are defending their idea of God's word.

You might wonder why religious groups don't just agree to disagree about God's word. Well, some groups actually do. Just look at the United States. The U.S. is a country made up of many different religions and cultures, but yet nobody goes to war over their different beliefs. There is acceptance amongst the religions, which is what makes America a great country to practice any religion that you want. After all, freedom of religion is in there constitution. Unfortunately, many of the Middle Eastern religions tend to stick with traditional beliefs even if it means going to war over them. They are less tolerant towards people's religious freedoms for this reason.

People believe in religion because it gives hope and meaning to their lives. Religious people developed an appreciation for the historical teachings of their religion. In other words, they appreciate what the founders of the religion had to go through in order to preach God's words to other people. What is really cool about religion is that there are so many different kinds of religions all around the world. Every area of the world has their own unique cultures, which enabled the people of those cultures to develop religions that fit their own way of life.

Hindu God Lord Ganesha with mother
Parvati

However, religions tend to change
somewhat over the years as cultures
begin to adapt to a changing world. A
perfect example of this is with the
Catholic Church and the Pope Francis.
Catholics used to view being gay as a sin
that would not get you into heaven. Now

the Pope is starting to show acceptance towards gay people, which is the first time any pope of the Catholic Church has ever done this. Why is he doing this? Since the United States and many European countries are starting to show acceptance towards gay people, it is a sign that the world's acceptance of gay people has changed. So, Pope Francis is trying to keep up with the times by allowing the church to accept gay people as well. Many religions make changes to their beliefs in order to gain more followers. Many might say this is a good thing, but changes to the original teachings of a religion could end up dividing it up into separate other groups, like in Hinduism.

What is God?

God is a word that has many different meanings. Overall, God is known as the "Supreme Being" that people pray to in their religions for hope and happiness. The way somebody thinks about God usually has to do with their religious beliefs. Some religions teach that God is a man that speaks to people. Other religions teach God cannot be seen, but only heard. The one thing all religions seem to agree on is that God is the creator of the world and the universe. God is the reason why all life exists on Earth, which means God created people.

A cross and a painting of baby Jesus with mother Mary

Most religions also agree that God's words are more important than anything. So, when God speaks to a prophet then we are all supposed to follow that prophet's message from God. Religions are different from each other because they all have their own unique teachings of God's message. Religions have all told their own stories about prophets receiving messages from God and these messages are different amongst all the religions. Also, the followers of a religion may end up interpreting God's words differently than other followers of the same faith. This causes those religions to break up and become many smaller religions, like how Catholicism and Protestant are smaller groups of Christianity. This kind of thing is what makes each individual religion unique from one another.

Religions have created many different names to identify God. Christians refer to God as "Jehovah," which you have probably heard associated with the term "Jehovah's Witnesses." Those are the Christians that walk around spreading the word of God to other people. In the Islamic religion, the Muslim followers refer to God as "Allah." There is no universal name for God that is used amongst all religions. Religious followers all call God something different because their teachings taught them different names. Despite the fact that most people don't see or hear God, they still choose to believe in him. After all, seeing does not necessarily mean believing. Religious followers have "faith" in their prophets and preachers. This means the followers trust that God spoke to these prophets without requiring any kind of proof other than their word. All it takes is for someone to believe in the power of God to know that he exists and is watching over their lives.

God is often associated with some kind of religion because many people need to have faith in order to believe in God. However, there are some people that can still believe in God without following a religion. After all, the true definition of God does not associate him with any one religion. God is just known as an all powerful force that created the world and all life as we know it. Since everyone is a part of that creation, they can choose to believe their own idea of what God is and the impact he has on our lives. You don't necessarily have to give God a name to believe in him either. As long as you know God exists then you will feel his power over your life.

Christianity

Christianity is one of the biggest religions of all time. There are over two billion Christian followers around the world and has merged with cultures in many different countries. Christianity first started in Jerusalem about 2000 years ago by a man who was first known as "Jesus of Nazareth." During this time period, Romans worshipped many gods and even allowed Judaists to worship their own god.

Jesus giving his sermons

However, a man named Jesus showed up
in Jerusalem around 30 A.D. to preach
God's word. Many of Jesus' followers
came to believe he was the actual son of
God and not just a prophet. These
followers ended up breaking many Roman
laws by not following Roman or Jewish
beliefs. This caused the Romans to arrest

Jesus and then execute him through crucifixion. This is a method of killing where somebody gets nailed to a cross and left there to bleed to death. However, Jesus' followers claimed to have seen him rise up from the cross three days later. This is what convinced them that Jesus was truly the son of God, which gave Jesus the added name of Christ. This word "Christ" means "chosen one" in Greek. This is why the followers of Jesus are known as Christians. The basic idea behind the Christian religion is that people's sins will be forgiven if they chose to love God and follow his teachings by becoming a Christian.

Fleeing Sodom and Gomorrah

The teachings of Christianity can be found in the Holy Bible, which is the Christian holy book. The bible contains what are known as the New Testament and Old Testament. The Old Testament was written years before Jesus ever came to exist. The writings of the Old Testament came from various Jewish people that wrote their ideas about how the world was created. These writings also include the story of the prophet, Moses, who received the Ten

Commandments from God. The New Testament is all about Jesus Christ and the sacrifices he made for our sins. Some Christian groups don't study both testaments. Christianity is so big that has been broken up into Roman Catholic, Protestant and Eastern Orthodox. Protestants will only accept the Old Testament as God's teachings whereas the others will consider both testaments as God's words.

The place where people go to pray to God is called a church. We have all heard about churches before. In other religions, these places of worship could be called temples or shrines. Church is the most popular term because Christianity is so well known by most people. Churches are usually big buildings made out of stone. They also have a big cross on top of the roof. The people inside churches that preach to Christian followers are called ministers or priests. These priests have a much deeper relationship with God than your average Christian. For one thing, priests can never get married nor have children because they have to fully devote their lives to God. It is almost like they are marrying God instead of a real person. Then they live the rest of their lives preaching God's words and helping other Christians keep their faith in him.

Islam

The Islamic religion is a very popular religion that has over one billion followers. It is just as popular as Catholicism, which has about the same number of followers. Islam was created during the year 570 in Saudi Arabia by a man named Muhammad. He is the prophet of the Islamic religion that was sent to deliver God's message to people. Unlike other religions, God did not come down and talk directly to the prophet. Instead, God sent an angel by the name of "Gabriel" to deliver his messages to Muhammad for him. Gabriel would constantly deliver messages to Muhammad and then Muhammad would preach these messages to other people. The most important message that Gabriel delivered to Muhammad was that there's only one true God in this world to worship. This God goes by the name of "Allah" and he is the creator of everything in this world.

Prophet Muhammad going to Medina

Muhammad continued to delivery Allah's messages to the people for many years. These messages taught people to live their lives in a way that would make Allah happy. After all, the number one objective of any Muslim is to make Allah happy. This is one of the five main rules of the Islamic religion that all Muslims live by. They must admit to themselves that Allah is the only god and that there are no other gods of worship.

The Kaaba, most sacred site in Islam

Muslims then have to pray five times throughout the day; like at dawn, noon, afternoon, sunset and at night. Muslims also have to be good to the poor and give them about 3% of their money, so that they can help them buy food for their families. It is very important to Muslims that they stay equal to the poor. On the ninth month of the calendar year, Muslims will not eat or drink in order to stay equal to the poor. This will also make Muslims feel more grateful for what they already have in their lives. Then the last rule Muslims must live by is to visit the sacred house known as Ka'bah, which is located in a city called Mecca. Muslims only have to visit Ka'bah at least once in their lifetime to satisfy that rule and make Allah happy.

Many religions have holy books as you probably already know. The holy book of the Islamic religion is called the Quran, or sometimes spelt Koran. This is the Muslim version of the Holy Bible that Christians follow. The Quran contains the word of God that Muslims believe in. These words, like the bible, tell people how to live their lives properly. Muslims have great respect for the Quran and its teachings. In fact, Muslims actually believe the Quran came from Allah himself. They believe every single letter and word in the Quran came from Allah without any alterations or variations. In other words, they don't think anyone else changed the text into something different than it originally was. Muslims hold every letter to be sacred because it came directly from Allah. When they read it they usually place the book on a wooden stand to hold it in place. Then they read in silence while memorizing Allah's words.

Hinduism

Hinduism is a 3000 year old religion, which makes it the oldest religion in the whole world. Someone that is a follower of Hinduism is commonly called a "Hindu." This was named after a popular river in India called the "Indus River." The Hindu religion was first created in India and has stayed there for thousands of years ever since. This is the reason why 80% of India's population believes in Hinduism. This is a pretty high percentage. Since over a billion people are living in India, which means that the majority of the world's population of Hindus live in India. Other countries where Hindus live include Nepal, Bangladesh, Indonesia, United States, Myanmar and United Kingdom.

Statue of Lord Balaji

Hinduism is a pretty unique religion that is kind of different than other religions. Hindus do not worship a single God, like Christians or Judaists. They also don't have just one person that created the religion, like prophets. Hinduism has so many different versions of itself, which means there are many groups of Hindus that have different beliefs from each other. The reason why the beliefs are different is because people interpret the teachings of Hinduism in different ways.

A Hindu holy man

These Hindu teachings do come out of the same holy book that all Hindus read which is called the "Vedas." Since Hinduism is the oldest religion in the world, Vedas is the oldest holy book in the world as well. This holy book instructs Hindu followers to encourage their friends and family to have faith in the religion. Vedas also serves as a guide for how to live your life the proper way. This is where many Hindus have a different interpretation because they are taught different stories from the book. Each story has their own unique version about how to live life and treat others. The only thing that all Hindus agree on is their belief in God, or otherwise known as Brahman (the Supreme Being). Hinduism is a polytheistic religion because Brahman is not seen as just one god that people can pray to in a church. Brahman is a god that lives inside everyone, so that he can help guide us on the right path in our lives. Hindus also believe Brahman is actually part of many other gods that are less powerful. The Hindu religion allows other smaller gods to be worshipped in order to discover the one true god, Brahman.

Despite Hindus having many different groups, they all still have four rules to live by. The first goal is to simply be good to other people. This could be feeding the homeless or giving somebody a ride that does not have a car. Another rule is to be kind to your parents and elders, but this has a different meaning than you may think. Hindus believe showing respect to your parents means that you are getting married and passing along the family name. So if you are a Hindu boy, then you are expected to get married after you become a man. The last goal is called "Karma," which many people have heard before. Karma means that if you show kindness to others then you will receive kindness in return. It also means if you treat people mean then you will be treated mean back. So, why not be kind then? That is the basic idea behind that rule. Hindus take these rules seriously and so they devote their entire lives to try to live up to them.

Buddhism

About 2500 years ago, a man named Siddhartha Gautama developed the religion of Buddhism. Siddhartha was a prince who lived a very rich and exciting life filled with luxury. You could say that he did not have too many worries. This all changed one day when he realized that bad things could still happen to him even though he was rich. After all, money cannot save you from getting sick or falling down and getting injured.

Image of Lord Buddha inside Bodh Gaya temple

Siddhartha decided to leave his luxurious lifestyle at his palace and go on a journey to meet four people. He wanted to meet a dead man, a sick man, an old man and a monk. Three of these people taught Siddhartha that he could not escape death, sickness or old age. Once he realized this, he met with the monk who encouraged him to become a holy person. This meant that Siddhartha had to abandon his life as a rich prince forever. As a holy person, Siddhartha was instructed by the monk to travel around the world seeking answers to two important questions; "What causes suffering?" and "Why do people suffer?" Everybody has wondered what the answers are to these questions, but Siddhartha used religious methods to find them. These methods included praying and meditating to find the answers. Once he was successful at learning the truth about suffering, he began telling others about it. People started referring to him as the enlightened one, which eventually led him to be called Buddha. It is from Buddha that the religion of Buddhism was developed.

Ancient statue of Lord Buddha in Patna museum

Buddhism is a religion that passes down the teachings of Buddha that are based on his original discoveries regarding the truth about suffering. These truths have been broken down into Noble Truths and Universal Truths. There are three Universal Truths that have to do with life in general. It teaches that everything in life changes and nothing ever stays the same, including your souls. In other words, people and their souls will change as time goes on. Another universal truth of Buddha teaches that possessions are not the key to happiness. Instead, you should just be happy that you are alive and healthy. The Noble Truths of Buddha are more about the suffering truths that he discovered. They explain that people are guaranteed to experience suffering in their lives no matter how rich or poor they are. Rich people suffer because they have too many possessions and have forgotten about the value of life in general. Poor people suffer because they spend so much time trying to obtain possessions. It is this human greed for material things that cause people to go to war with each other and kill each other. Buddha teaches that greed erases your ability to understand the value of human life. However, if you lead an honest life by working hard and not hurting other people then you will be happy forever. You won't even feel sad or angry about anything in your life. Buddha guarantees eternal happiness if you follow his ways of living life.

Atheism

Atheism is a growing trend in this world. The word "atheism" means "no God," which means anyone who is an atheist is somebody that does not believe in God's existence. Many people get confused as to what atheists actually are or what they believe in. Often times the word God gets associated with religion. So, people think that if you don't believe in God then you are not associated with any religion. In actuality, religion and God are two different things. God is known as the creator of the universe, the world and all life as we know it. Religion is simply defined as a set of beliefs regarding the creation of the world and the purpose of our existence.

Paul Henri Thiry a French-German author, philosopher and encyclopedist in the 18th-century was an atheist

Most religions use God as the explanation for our existence, which is why God and religion are so often seen together. However, atheism can still be called a religion because it represents a set of beliefs about the world just like any traditional religion. The only difference is that they don't use God as the explanation for it. Instead, they use logic, scientific evidence and scientific theories as a belief system. This means that atheists study scientific books instead of holy books to understand the world. Science is actually the main reason why people started becoming atheists. Atheism only began around two hundred years ago after science started getting more popular with people. Before that, pretty much everybody had some kind of other religious beliefs that involved God or some spiritual being that guided them in their lives. Atheism is one of the first "religions" to not have any kind of spiritual being in its teachings.

Many people of other religions don't consider atheism to be a true religion because there is no church or God associated with it. They also don't consider atheism to be a belief system, but in actuality it is. In fact, the population of atheists is growing by the day. The number is getting so big that atheists actually gather together now in order to celebrate life. This gathering is similar to a traditional church gathering on Sunday, but instead of celebrating God they celebrate living. They celebrate the power we all have inside to change our lives and make our dreams come true. Atheist gatherings are not about preaching to people that God does not exist or that other religions are wrong in believing in God. In fact, Atheist gatherings do not even mention God at all. They just talk about how we all have control over our own destiny and that we only have each other to depend on. The only problem right now with "atheist churches" is that there are not a lot of them. They only recently began in California and are slowly spreading across the United States. Unfortunately, the majority of atheists still do not have a church or gathering they can go to like they do in other religions. However, this will change as more people choose atheism as their religion.

Sikhism

Sikhism is a religion that was started 500 years ago in Punjab, which is a region in North India. A man by the name of Guru Nanak started this religion in the 1600s as a way of creating peace between rivaling religious groups. During this time in India, there were only Muslims and Hindus living there. They were two religious groups that did not like each other very much because they each believed in God differently. So, they would go to war over their religious differences. This inspired Guru Nanak to preach about religious acceptance by not hurting each other through violence. He even began to explain to people that God did not care about the little differences in people's religious beliefs. All he cares about is that you believe in God and not hurt each other over your beliefs.

Guru Nanak

The Guru was able to convince some people about God's word while others still doubted him. Fortunately, Guru Nanak was able to reach enough people that would continue to preach his words after he died. The Sikh leadership would keep getting passed down to more people called "Gurus."

After Guru Nanak died, there were nine more gurus that followed after him. Eventually, Sikh followers decided to stop making new gurus and to instead put all of the teachings into a holy book. Sikhs could then just read from the book rather than listen to somebody preach the teachings to them. The holy book of the Sikh religion is known as "Guru Granth Sahib". The Guru Granth Sahib is the holiest of all Sikh religious texts. It is a collection of hymns and qualities describing God along with the teachings of the 10 Sikh Gurus.

If somebody wants to become a Sikh they have to read this entire book and try to memorize it. The basic concepts of this book are similar to the teachings of other holy books. The Guru Granth Sahib basically tells people to believe in God and to treat everybody equally because God does the same. This means Sikhs have to live an honest life by helping other people who are less fortunate and never stealing. In fact, Sikhs are encouraged to work a job that will help others in their community and not hurt anyone. Sikhs are not even allowed to hurt themselves either. This means they cannot take drugs, drink alcohol or smoke cigarettes. They have to keep their bodies pure at all times because this will enable them to be able to help others without any setbacks. Sikhs are so committed to helping people that they gather in a temple of worship, known as Gurudwara, to organize ways of helping people. This temple is like their church because they pray and worship their God here. However, it is different than a traditional church because they do more than just pray. The Sikhs talk to each other, solve problems and even eat foods.

A Sikh temple is called a Gurudwara

Baptized Sikhs wear a turban on their head to show mark of respect and devotion to God by allowing it to grow naturally and never cutting it. They also keep a comb, wear bracelet on their wrist, and wear a special undergarment and keep a dagger or sword called "kirpan" with them. They are kept for symbolic purposes.

Judaism

The religion of Judaism goes back 4000 years, which makes it the oldest religion out of any other. It was started in the Middle East by a man named "Abraham." He was the first person to preach the idea that there was only one God to follow and worship. This was a new concept to people in the Middle East because they were used to worshipping many different gods instead of just one.

Star of David is a hexagram used as a Jewish symbol

The followers of Abraham who began believing in a single God were called Hebrews. Abraham continued to gain more followers throughout the remainder of his life. After he died, his children and grandchildren preached the same message that Abraham preached when he was alive. These descendents of Abraham became known as Israelites, which was a name taken from one of Abraham's grandchildren. The Hebrews believed that God would watch over them and keep them safe as long as they followed God's rules. In return for God's kindness of watching over them, the Hebrews decided to travel to other lands and spread God's message in the hopes of gaining more followers. They were able to do this for a little while, but when they reached Egypt their fate changed quickly. The Egyptian authorities did not take kindly to the Hebrews spreading their religion to the Egyptian people. So, the Hebrews got forced into slavery for their preaching.

Prophet Moses in the middle with Aaron
and Hur

God was not about to let his followers
stay in slavery for very long. So, he kept
his promise of watching over his Hebrew
people by sending a man named "Moses"
to free the enslaved Hebrews, which he
did successfully. God was very pleased
with Moses, so he entrusted him with the
written laws of the land. These were
God's laws and Moses was sent to teach

these laws of the land to other people. God gave Moses these laws in the form of tablets, which became known as the Ten Commandments. Some of these commandments are the basis of the laws that we have in modern day society, such as don't steal and don't kill. The commandments also mention that you cannot lie or care about possessions; however, these are not modern day laws. Hebrew followers have to follow all of the commandments in order to gain acceptance by God. The Ten Commandments were eventually rewritten into a holy book that now goes by the name of "Torah." The Hebrew followers are required to read the Torah and memorize all of God's teachings in it.

Judaism is still a popular religion around the world. The two countries where it is most popular are Israel and the United States. According to a recent survey, there are over six million Jewish people in Israel and over five million Jewish people in the United States. Since there are almost fourteen million Jewish people in the entire world, the majority of the followers reside in these two countries. Over the years Judaism split up into three smaller groups that have various interpretations of the Torah. There are the Orthodox Jews, Reform Jews and Conservative Jews. They all still believe in God, but they just have different ideas on how certain religious customs should be carried out. Orthodox Jews follow the Torah completely, Conservative Jews believe the Torah needs amending for modern purposes and Reform Jews think men and women should sit together at the dinner table.

Bahai Faith

The Bahai faith is a religion that was first created in Persia, which is now called Iran. Many of the religions in this book are many hundreds or even thousands of years old. The Bahai faith is only about 170 years old because it was started in 1844. It all began when a man, Siyyid Ali Muhammad Shírází, had predicted that a prophet would come and deliver God's message. Sure enough, a prophet did show up and delivered a message about everyone needing to find peace with each other. This prophet went by the name of Baha'u'llah. Baha'u'llah had an objective to unite the people of the world along with all the religions of the world. He wanted to put an end to fighting and arguing amongst people, so that peace and harmony could take over the world. This would create a world that had now racism, no prejudices and no discrimination. Unfortunately, he did not succeed in his message and ended up persecuted by Muslim leaders. But, this did not stop his followers because they made it their mission to spread the word of God all around the world. As of today, there are a little more than five million followers of the Bahai Faith.

The followers of Bahai only believe in one God just like other monotheistic religions. However, these followers don't see God as someone or something that you can know. Instead, they believe God becomes a part of the prophets that get sent by him to deliver his messages. These are known as "manifestations of God." The way people get to see God is through the prophets that spread his messages. These are the beliefs and teachings of the Bahai faith. When Bahai followers practice their religion it usually involves praying to God in private. There are no priests or reverends who preach the teachings of the religion. Followers have to study the teachings from books or learn them from other followers. The reason for this is because everybody is considered equal in the eyes of God. So, you can't have a priest or some holy person who is supposed to be "holier" than everyone else. The followers are all told they are equal and so they must keep up their own faith. In the entire world, there are eight Bahai Houses of Worship. One of the grand ones is located in Delhi, India. But, followers are not required to go there to keep up their faith. Also people from all faiths can go there.

The Bahai Lotus Temple in Delhi, India

The Bahai faith does not have a traditional holy book like many other religions. Their teachings simply come from a collection of sacred texts that were written by prophets over the years. These texts were then reprinted into books, so that people all around the world could study them. The worldliness of this religion is what makes it so unique. Most religions are associated with certain cultures or particular regions of the world. Bahai followers see themselves as citizens of the world, so they will have discussions with people from all cultural and religious backgrounds.

Confucianism

Confucianism is a very interesting religion because its followers, known as Confucians, do not worship a God or read the teachings of a God. Instead, they follow the teachings of an actual man who lived about 2500 years ago named Confucius. He lived in ancient China, which was a time when people were constantly at war. His goal was to convince people that showing kindness to others was the best thing for society. It would make society beautiful and there would be no more wars. Confucius devoted his entire life to showing others the right way to behave and how to live their lives properly. Besides being kind, you also had to be respectful towards your ancestors and avoid getting upset with people for whatever reason. Confucius created five virtues, or ways of living, that people need to follow based on these ideas. The virtues are kindness, sobriety, righteousness, trustworthiness and wisdom. If you follow these virtues then you will be to make contact with the spiritual forces of nature and they will keep you happy forever.

In modern times, there are about five million people in the world that are Confucians. Most of these people live in China where the religion originated. Confucians do not have a holy book like other religions do. Instead, they have to read from a series of scriptures that are made up of poems, rituals, historical content and quotations. These were written by ancient Confucians and preserved over time to be studied by future Confucians. As for a place of worship, there are no traditional churches where you pray to a God. The closest thing Confucians have to churches is temples; however, these temples are primarily used as a place to honor the dead. Ceremonies take place in these temples to allow dead Confucians to be one with the spirits. This is a spiritual world that resembles heaven, but it is not to be confused with the heaven that is found in Christianity. Confucians see heaven as a spiritual world for their people. In fact, they often think of this heaven as their own God. This is not a God that takes the shape of a powerful being, but a force that created the virtues in which Confucians have inside of them. You have to remember that Confucianism is not about worshipping a God, so that he will bless you for being good in your life. Confucianism is more about studying the ways of being a better person and then knowing the rewards that come along with it.

Confucius

There is something called "Jen," which teaches Confucians that their own happiness depends on the happiness of those that are around them. So, if you treat people terribly and are mean to them then you will feel bad about yourself. On the other hand, if you show kindness and generosity to people then you will feel good about yourself. This is the power of Jen and it is what Confucians long to have in their lives. That way after they die they can become one of the spirits that guides living Confucians towards their destiny.

Jainism

Jainism is a very old religion and nobody knows the exact time it was created. Some people believe it was created around the same time as Buddhism, which was created 2500 years ago. In the whole world, there are five million followers of Jainism. These people are commonly referred to as Jains. We do know that Jainism was originally developed in India, which is where many of the modern day followers reside. Anyone else in the world who is a Jain was probably related to someone that immigrated out of India.

Lord Mahavira in deep meditation

Jainism was one of the first religions to not have a God or Supreme Being to worship. Jains believe that the universe and everything in it including things like matter, time, space and everything else has always existed. Jain teachings are all about being kind to other people and not hurting them with violence. Jains follow a path of non-violence towards all living things, a philosophy called Ahimsa. This idea first came about by a wealthy prince named Mahavira. He was not big on possessions or material things, despite the fact that he was rich. He figured out that having a spiritual connection with people and the rest of the world was a better way to live life.

A Jain temple

Once he convinced other people of this, they began following in his footsteps. This ultimately led to the creation of Jainism and the followers that began living their life in the same spiritual way. What is neat about living this spiritual life is that you are not afraid of death. In fact, Jains cannot wait to get to the end of their life because they will be in Moksha. This place of Moksha is where all Jains want to get to because it allows their mind and body to be completely freed from the world. The only way a Jain can reach Moksha is by following the teachings of Jainism. This means they have to be kind to people and not commit acts of violence. If they are able to do this successfully then they will not be re-born into a new life. However, if Jains do hurt other people then they will not reach Moksha and will be reborn again.

Jainism believes in showing kindness towards all living things, not just people. You are not even allowed to step on an insect that is crawling on the ground. If you do, then you won't reach Moksha. Jains believe all living things have souls of their own, which includes people, animals, insects and even plants. Jains cannot kill or destroy any of these things or else they will be considered evil in the eyes of their people. You have to be a very devoted follower of the religion in order to be this perfect. Some Jains typically walk around with a broom and sweep the ground they walk on because they are afraid of stepping on a bug. Some Jains even wear facial masks to avoid accidently eating or swallowing an insect that is flying in the air. If you ever visit a Jain follower then you have to carry out these same traditions or else they will not want anything to do with you.

Zoroastrianism

Zoroastrianism is a 2000 year old religion that began in Iran, which was called "Persia" back in those days. During this time, the people of Persia were not at peace with each other. This encouraged a prophet, Zoroaster (also called Zarathustra), to try and help people get along better with each other. So, Zarathustra began preaching to people about the benefits of kindness and generosity. Some of the people began following what Zarathustra had to say. These people became known as "Parsis," which were increasing in size as Zarathustra continued to preach his words of peace. However, this new loving society was soon destroyed after a group of bad tribesmen began killing each other. The killing was so bad that Zarathustra was unable to bring any more peace to Persia. So, he convinced his remaining followers to move away from Persia in order to avoid getting killed by these violent tribesmen.

The Faravahar (also called Frawahr) is a symbol of Zoroastrianism

Zoroastrianism is a monotheistic religion, which means the followers only worship one God. Zoroastrians call this God "Ahura Mazda" and they believe he created all life in this world. However, they also believe there is an evil spirit called "Angra Mainyu." Zoroastrians blame this evil spirit for all the pain and suffering that goes on in the world. But one day, there is supposed to be a giant battle between Ahura Mazda and Angra Mainyu. They are hoping that the good God will win and bring peace back to this Earth.

In the mean time, Zoroastrians have to make the choice themselves to be good or to be evil. The amount of goodness that a Zoroastrian has inside of them gets determined when they die. Instead of just going to heaven or hell right away, Zoroastrians have to cross a bridge to get to heaven after they die. The ability to get across the bridge is determined by the amount of goodness that person had while they were alive. If they did a lot of good deeds then they will be able to cross the bridge successfully and get into heaven. However, if they were evil and were bad to people then they will fall off the bridge. The place below the bridge is where hell lies, so if you fall off the bridge then you will go to hell. So basically, an evil person will be punished by ending up in hell for not being able to cross the bridge.

Symbols are very important to Zoroastrians. They are used to represent places and personalities. For example, fire is one of the most important symbols to Zoroastrians. It is a symbol used on all of their temples of worship, which are commonly called fire temples. Zoroastrians believe that fire is a representation of truth and righteousness. The fire temples have priests who keep fires burning inside of the temple at all times. That way truth and righteousness can stay within the temple. Another symbol is the color white, which represents purity in a person. Zoroastrians wear white shirts and pray with a white belt in order to show this. The purity means they are devoting themselves to their religion and the people of their community.

When a Zoroastrian dies, their body is placed on the roof of a building called the "tower of silence." This is a circular tower made out of stone where birds fly down to eat the dead bodies of the Zoroastrians. This tradition exists because Zoroastrians do not want their followers to rot in the ground after they die. Also they do not want to pollute the good creation by God.

Shinto

Shinto is a Japanese word that means "way of the gods." This was a religion that was developed in ancient Japan around 3500 years ago, which makes it even older than Hinduism and Judaism. Despite the meaning of the name, Shintoism is not about worshipping gods. Instead, Shinto followers worship spirits that are called "kami." They believe kami lives inside all natural things on Earth, such as people, plants, animals, water, mountains and stones. They even believe kami is inside of dead people.

This is Fugin (also called Futen or Kami-no-Kaze) - one of the Gods of the Shinto religion. He is seen carrying a large bag of wind on his shoulders

Shintoism uses shrines instead of churches as their places of worship. These shrines are placed in beautiful landscaped areas that represent the very best of nature. These shrines contain Shinto priests that can be either female or male. Shinto shrines are easy to recognize because they are marked with a unique archway that is called "torii." This archway is very special to the Shinto followers because it separates the outside world from their sacred world inside the shrine. There are 80,000 of these shrines that can be found all over Japan. Every year the Shinto followers have a festival where they celebrate the kami spirit by having delicious foods and drinks. Throughout the rest of the year the Shintoists are pretty clean in what they eat. Shinto followers are actually big believers into purity, which means they like to stay as clean as possible. This involves constantly washing their mouths and hands, so that they stay pure. When Shintoists pray they hang up a series of wooden tablets that have Shinto prayers already written on them. These are hung up in a special prayer hall of the shrine. The priests will summon the Shinto followers by ringing a large bell, which is also supposed to summon the kami spirit. The worshipper will then offer the kami either money or rice. After that, the worshipper bows and claps twice as a way of welcoming the kami to the prayer hall.

Shintoism is still very popular in Japan because it has over five million followers. You may wonder how so many followers could fit inside 80,000 shrines. Well, the truth is you don't have to visit a shrine to worship the kami spirit. Shinto followers are allowed to worship in their homes and even at the place of work. All they have to do is offer the kami spirit some tea and rice as a peace offering. They place this offering on top of a special shelf, which is called "Godshelf." Even though the word "God" is in this word, do not think of it in the traditional way. The kami spirit is what Shintoists worship, so it is the closest thing to a God that they have.

When Shintoists pray to the kami spirit they usually address their prayers towards the ancestors of their family. After all, they believe kami lives within their dead ancestors and so they want to make sure their spirits are at peace. In Japan, you will find a lot of Buddhists practicing Shintoism along with their own religion because they both share similar beliefs.

Wicca

Wicca is a religion that is focused more on spirituality and less on one Supreme Being or God. Wiccans get their spirituality from the seasons of the earth, like summer, winter, fall and spring. They believe the weather and natural forces of each season cause spirits to make contact with us. Wiccans even hold festivals during lunar and solar eclipses because they believe this is when the spirits are trying to communicate with the world. All things that pertain to nature are important to Wiccans. That is why many Wiccans try to live as natural as possible, which means they sleep outdoors and eat foods that grow from the ground.

The moon has powerful influences on all living things. In the Wicca belief system, the moon is considered as a Goddess or the female part of divinity

Historians believe that this belief system was first developed in Europe thousands of years ago before Christianity came to exist. Wicca was not a religion back in those days, but the spirituality concept was. Wicca did not actually become a religion until the early 20th century in England. Still, the majority of people did not think of it as a traditional religion. It was considered to be a "witchcraft religion" because of its religious rituals that deal in magic instead of prayers. These magic rituals are how Wiccans make things happen. Many people misunderstand the word "magic" because they often associate it with a person that has magical powers. Wiccans do not believe any one person has the power of magic. Instead, the Wiccans believe the spirits of the world will make things happen for them if they are summoned through a ritual. This ritual is usually conducted in a sacred circle where spells get cast. Most Wiccans use this magic to do good deeds, like healing the sick and ridding the community of evil spirits. This kind of magic has been nicknamed "white magic." On the flip side, there are also Wiccans who use their magic rituals for evil purposes. This could be magic that kills someone or causes them great harm. This kind of magic is called "black magic."

Wiccans do not have a holy book or any kind of sacred text where they get their teachings from. The reason why many other religions have holy books is because they had prophets who claimed they spoke with God. Then those prophets or their ancestors wrote God's message into a book. The Wiccan religion does not have prophets in its history or anyone who claimed they made contact with God. The only types of leaders that Wiccans have are priests, who have to go through many years of spiritual rituals to get accepted as one. Sometimes even women become priests, which are known as priestesses. All Wiccan priests are much respected and are considered teachers of the Wiccan religion. These are the people who young Wiccans lookup to in order to gain spiritual knowledge about their religion. Most importantly, the priests help Wiccans get in touch with their spirituality, which is supposed to help them experience the true meaning of life. All Wiccans believe that it is possible to achieve this goal.

Shamanism

Shamanism is a belief system developed by the Turks and Mongols of the 16th century in Northern Asia. Many people don't like to call Shamanism a religion because it deals with spirits and magic. Shamanism is very similar to Wicca because they both mix spirituality with medicine that heals people. However, someone who is a shaman is more than just a follower of this religion. They actually have a special relationship with the spiritual forces that surround them. Shamanism is all about believing that the world is filled with invisible spirits and other forces that influence people's lives. These spiritual forces allow shaman people to diagnose a person's illness and then cure it. Shamans do not use any kind of traditional medicine or treatments to make this happen. They are believed to have special contact with the spirit world that is responsible for curing and causing illnesses. This allows shamans to cure people that are sick, but it also gives them the power to cause illnesses as well.

That's right the shamans can give people illnesses just as easily as they can take them away. The good shamans that heal people are known as "medicine men "and the evil shamans that make people sick are called "witch doctors."

Shamanism does not contain followers that gather into a church or shrine in order to worship the spirits. Shamans communicate with the spirit world alone by going into trances through deep meditation. In a way, this is the shaman version of praying and going to church because they do both through this meditation. The church they go to is the "spiritual realm" that they enter in their minds, so that they can come up with solutions to problems in their community. A person can believe in the magic and spiritual side of Shamanism, but in order to become a Shaman you must go through a series of spiritual rituals to prove that you have contact with spirits. Shamans will then become what are known as "intermediaries" between the spiritual world and the living world. In other words, they are the messengers of both worlds that treat the illnesses of both sides. You might be wondering how a soul could have an illness, but the shamans believe that souls can be misguided or lost. Shamans believe the misguided soul of an ill person is the reason why they are sick. So, what the shamans do is they fix their soul to treat their sickness. Once the soul has been mended, the person will be cured.

A Shaman with his magic drum

In modern day society, Shamanism can mostly be found in Asian countries. However, the population of shamans is still extremely low. Most people think of

Shamanism as nothing more than a fantasy religion because of the magic and healing aspect of it. In western society, the only way people hear about it is through works of fiction. Video gamers that have played the game "World of Warcraft" will be very familiar with Shamanism because there are shamans in the game. In real life, there are still some people in the world that believe in the magic to heal their sickness. These are usually people in poor countries that do not have any other hope. Whether the magic is real or not is still up for debate.

Taoism

Taoism is a 2500 year old religion that was developed by a Chinese philosopher and poet named Lao Tze. This philosopher just happened to live during the same time period as Confucius, who is a better known Chinese philosopher. However, Lao Tze's journey towards religion was a little different. Lao Tze didn't just preach his ideas to the people as soon as he got them. Instead, he decided to leave his job and explore the western region of China in order to meet with a guardian. The only mode of transportation he had was an ox that he rode on. He eventually made it to a mountain pass where the guardian was waiting for him. Then Lao Tze wrote down his philosophies about life onto scrolls. Basically, the writings teach that being good towards others will give you a better life. This means you cannot kill, steal, lie, drink alcohol or cheat on your wife. These scrolls were turned into a sacred book known as Daodejing. When you see statues of Lao Tze he is usually inside an ox, which is suppose to symbolize his journey to the mountain pass where the religion was born.

Yin and Yang symbol

Taoism is still a popular religion thousands of years after it was first created. In the modern world there are over five million followers of Taoism, who are called "Taoists." This religion is most popular in Asian countries, like Vietnam, Japan, China, Taiwan and Malaysia. Taoism is often combined with other religions, like Buddhism and especially

Confucianism. What these three religions have in common is they all do not worship any one particular God. Instead, they are spiritual religions that follow the teachings written by philosophers instead of God. For example, a Taoist believes that if they are good to people then they will get to live with Tao in the afterlife for all eternity. Again, they think of Tao as their God and so they believe he will merge with your soul if you follow his teachings. Nowadays, Taoists believe Tao actually is responsible for the forces of nature; like the stars, sun, moon and ocean tides. Taoists actually worship these natural forces the same way other religions worship their God.

Terracotta soldier with his horse. These terracotta figures were made by the knowledge given by Tao alchemists

Many people have probably seen the symbol for Taoism without even realizing what it meant. Taoism uses the Yin Yang symbol, which is a circle with two black and white halves that have opposite colored dots. This is supposed to represent two opposing forces that find harmony together. Taoists are all about making bad things good by doing good deeds. The way a Taoist prepares himself to be good is by meditation. There is a specific kind of meditation that you have probably heard of called "Tai Chi." This meditation is very popular and is still used today. It involves slow moving exercises that help control the body and mind. Tai Chi can actually be used as both a form of meditation and a form of physical exercise. So, you can even lose weight while doing it! The person who created Tai Chi is not thoroughly documented, although historians believe a man named Zhang Sanfeng invented it. He was a 12th century Taoist, so he was born many years after Taoism was first created.

Message from the author

The religions mentioned in this book are the oldest and most popular religions of the modern world. You might be thinking that all religions are old and that prophets no longer exist anymore. However, there are new religions being created in our modern day society all the time. The two newest religions that have gone main stream are Mormonism and Scientology. They both have their own founders and their own set of beliefs that they have preached to people. Overall, these religions are no different than the religions described in this book.

It is just up to you to decide which belief system makes sense in your mind. When you find a religion that appeals to you then follow it with all your heart. Just remember there is no wrong choice for a religion. As long as you don't hurt anybody else or yourself, then any belief system is good if it helps guide you in your life. Perhaps, you may want to create your own religion with a belief system that you feel is appropriate for society and the modern world. By studying religions, you can get a basic idea of the power it can have on people and how much it can help them in their lives. Hopefully, you learned from this book that helping people is the best way to get them to listen to you. It proves you're sincere and that you are not trying to hurt anybody. That is how the prophets were able to convince people to join their religions. You could be a prophet to.

More books

Hinduism For Kids: Beliefs And Practices

India For Kids: Amazing Facts About India

Indian Religions For Kids

Mahatma Gandhi For Kids And Beginners

Made in United States
North Haven, CT
21 February 2022